D. P Howe

Howe's Science of Language or Seven Hour System of

Grammar

D. P Howe

Howe's Science of Language or Seven Hour System of Grammar

ISBN/EAN: 9783337085001

Printed in Europe, USA, Canada, Australia, Japan

Cover: Foto ©Paul-Georg Meister /pixelio.de

More available books at **www.hansebooks.com**

HOWE'S

SCIENCE OF LANGUAGE,

OR

SEVEN-HOUR SYSTEM

OF

GRAMMAR.

BY PROF. D. P. HOWE,

OF THE UNION COLLEGE, BOSTON, MASS.

MANCHESTER, N. H.:

C. F. Livingston's Printing House,

SPRING STREET.

1870.

INTRODUCTION.

——:o:——

This little work has been published at the urgent and repeated request of persons of all shades of education in every State of the Union, from Maine to Florida. It is designed to meet the requirements of a class of persons, immersed in business pursuits, entirely cut off from the advantages and influence of the School Room, and whose opportunities of an educational developement in this particular are at an end. With an experience of more than thirty years in the art of teaching, and a familiar acquaintance with the views of nearly a thousand authors, the writer is enabled to form an opinion of his own. He is satisfied that one of the greatest obstacles to the understanding of Grammar, is the scattered arrangement of thought, as exhibited in the Text Books of the present day. The writer has endeavored to remove this difficulty, by concentrating the scattered fragments of the Science, and bringing into measurable compass all that is practically useful for every-day life. His arrangement in this particular is entirely original. Every gem of thought, every idea of value, and every excellence in the Science worthy of attention, he has retained, while the profuse surplus nonsense, the literary brushwood, and the metaphysical, perplexing subtleties of the Text Books, which have ever obscured the Science, he has given to the winds. These may be interesting to the Professor of Logic, but to the great mass, who desire simple knowledge, they are absolutely valueless. What he has retained must be carefully read and digested, and if put into practice will constitute the scholar ; what he has omitted is not worth the looking after. To the uneducated, yet ambitiqus person, this little work will prove a particular friend ; for by it, independent of all previous knowledge or preparatory fitness, he can climb from the A. B. C. of the Science to its most practical highths ; while the profound student already famous for his attainments in search after knowledge, will find many bewildering and perplexing difficulties explained and simplified.

The author's discovery of the *limited governing power* of the Transitive Verbs and Prepositions, startling as it may be, has met with universal approval and recognition, from every intelligent, unprejudiced scholar who has heard it. With this fact before the mind, the education of *years* is diminished into as many *minutes*, and that which before was wild, immeasurable, and incomprehensible confusion, is now a perfect simplicity. Those SEVEN WORDS, as contrasted with the 30,000 Nouns and the 60 Pronouns of the text books, are worthy of being written in *letters of lightning* across the heavens for all Christendom to witness, as being the only words in the English language, under the control of the governing powers named, in which a grammatical error can be made. He might point with pleasure also to the simplicity of the suspended vibrating *s*, securing agreement between the Verb and the Noun, which has proved the delight of thousands ; and to his exposition of the Subjunctive Mood and Prepositions, all of the utmost value to the Platform Speaker, the Clergyman, or the Senator. Fifteen minutes' attention to any one of these will protect any intelligent person from erring once in a life time.

In conclusion, any one desiring to speak or write correctly, can accomplish what he wishes, by giving this little work one week's study; and he will, in this short time, attain to a greater perfection, a more thorough knowledge of the English language, than he could secure by many tedious years of study, from the common text books of the country. Should his efforts to simplify this most important of all branches of Science, meet to some extent the literary necessities of the *adult population* of America, and prove, as intended, the right-hand friend of the Self-Student, the writer's most ardent wishes will have been accomplished.

BOSTON, MASS., March, 1870.

GRAMMAR.

GRAMMAR is the art of expressing our thoughts correctly, in speaking or writing.

ENGLISH LANGUAGE.

The ENGLISH LANGUAGE is divided into nine Parts of Speech: *Article, Noun, Adjective, Pronoun, Verb, Adverb, Preposition, Conjunction* and *Interjection.*

☞ By these *nine divisions,* science has spanned our language, as a magnificent river is spanned by a bridge, and its rippling waters flow through the several arches.

THE NOUN

IS THE PRINCIPAL PART OF SPEECH.

———

Of the nine parts of speech, the Noun is the principal one. Like the sun in the Solar System, it takes the position of centre, round which the remaining eight parts of speech revolve as mere satellites, taking the secondary office of modifiers:

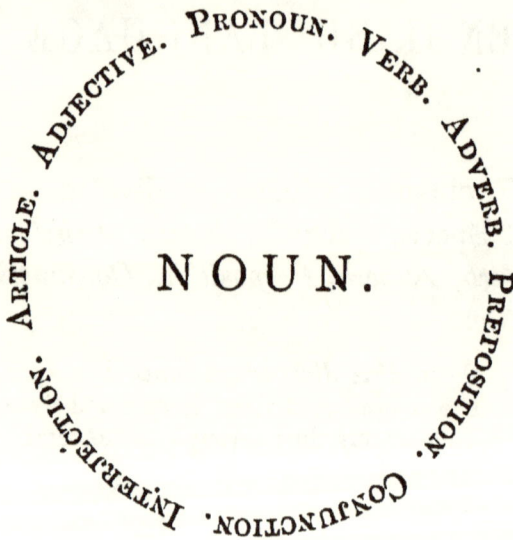

PRONOUN. VERB. ADVERB. PREPOSITION. CONJUNCTION. INTERJECTION. ARTICLE. ADJECTIVE.

NOUN.

☞ Thus, the Articles point to the Nouns, or to the objects which they represent: the Adjectives give them character; the Pronouns are their substitutes; the Verbs state something about them; the Adverbs tell how their actions are done; the Prepositions show their relative position; the Conjunctions couple them together, and the Interjections express their emotion.

ARTICLES.

ARTICLES limit nouns; or, an Article is a word that points out nouns and limits them; as, *A* star; *an* organ; *the* sun.

☞ There are two Articles, A and The, and these may be considered in their use, as the two *Index Fingers* of the English language. A, derived from *ane* (one) of the Anglo Saxon, means one, and is therefore necessarily used in the singular number; as, A *mountain;* a *flower;* a *city.*

☞ Anterior to the Conquest, *ane* was in universal use : as, *ane* man; *ane* town; *ane* apple; *ane* orchard. At a later day *ane* lost the final *e*, and An (an-e) like to its predecessor, took the full circle of the Nouns of the language, irrespective of Vowel or Consonant sounds; as, An boy; an man; an apple; an ornament. Finally, as time rolled on, the *n* was removed, and A stands to-day, the modern Indefinite Article of the language.

☞ For the sake of euphony the removed *n* is sometimes recalled to coalesce with A, as, *An* apple; *an* instrument.

This necessity produced the following simple rule, assented to by all grammarians : *Vowel sounds* require *An* before them; *Consonant sounds*, A.

VOWEL SOUNDS.	CONSONANT SOUNDS.
An *army.*	A *butterfly.*
An *enemy.*	A *casket.*
An *instrument.*	A *delicacy.*
An *officer.*	A *foreigner,*
An *umbrella.*	A *giant,* &c.

Words commencing with a *silent h* give a vowel sound; as, *H*onest, *h*onorable; Those

The sharp sound of u as it is found in *unity* is made by *y* or *yu*; hence as *y* is having the *h sounded*, when a consonant whenever it the *accent* is on the *second syllable*, give only an imperfect consonant sound, and hence, by general consent, both are placed among the words having vowel sounds; as,— begins a word or syllable, words having this sound are placed by universal consent and the best authority, among those words requiring the Article A; as,—

An *h*onest man.	A unit.
An hotél incident.	A euphony.
An Havána letter.	A ewer.
An heróic action.	A useful boy.
An heréditary disease.	A university.

☞ THE is called the Definite Article because it *defines* and points out definitely; as, *The* Creation, *the* Flood and *the* Crucifixion, are *the* three great facts of biblical history.

> *The* great, *the* gay, shall they partake,
> *The* heaven that thou alone can'st make?

☞ Unlike the Indefinite Article A, the Definite Article *The*, undergoes *no grammatical change*, but may be used indiscriminately before Nouns in the *singular number*, and those in the *plural number*, and before *vowel sounds*, as well as *consonant sounds*; as, The mountain, or, the mountains; the *a*rmy, or, the *n*avy.

☞ Attention to the preceding arrangements, and the practice of them in speaking or writing, will, so far as the Articles go, constitute the grammarian; but to follow this or any other part of speech into *every sentence*, and show its use and application to it, would not be any more a sensible act, than attempting to fix beforehand the undulations of the eagle's wing in its flight through the heavens, or to trace the movements of a ship, in all its angular and meandering courses through the trackless ocean. All who try it fail; and yet it is this unnecessary *chasing of words through the language*, that fills to satiety the text books of the present day, and makes the science, which might otherwise appear interesting and attractive, a complete *metaphysical puzzle*, and a *hateful absurdity* to the student.

NOUNS.

Nouns are names; or, a Noun is the *name* of any person, place, object, or idea; as, *William, London, garden, happiness.* This, or any other definition, gives but a feeble idea of this part of speech; and as the Noun forms the base upon which the whole superstructure of the English language is beautifully and permanently erected, we are compelled to view it in all its interesting features, and follow it to its utmost limits.

☞ As it is entirely impossible to make use of objects themselves in speaking and writing, we use the *names.* The necessity of this is obvious; for no person can place a continent or village upon his tongue, neither can he with a pen dip up the ocean or even a city reservoir for the accommodation of his correspondents. He can, however, speak the *name,* continent or village, and with similar ease write the *name,* ocean or reservoir, with his pen. Hence the *name* is all the speaker or writer has to do with, which accounts for the universal application of the Noun.

. B

☞ To grasp the Noun in its immense variety, we must give our imagination the greatest freeness of action, and trace, so far as we are able, the works of creation through limitless space. Remembering, that there is nothing in nature so large or so diminutive, so distant or so near, so holy or so impure, that will not come under the immediate control of the tongue or pen, and form a subject of conversation or correspondence.

☞ If we glance at the heavens, we find the whole firmament full of sparkling orbs, scattered like glittering gold-dust from horizon to horizon. We find the sun, the moon, the planets, and the stars attracting our attention, and instinctively calling our aspirations to the great Author of creation. In this spirit Addison penned the following inimitable lines, which may be grammatically, as well as morally, considered:

> The spacious *firmament* on high,
> With all the blue ethereal *sky ;*
> And spangled *heavens*, a shining *frame*,
> Their great ORIGINAL proclaim.
> The unwearied *sun* from *day* to *day*,
> Doth his CREATOR'S *power* display ;
> And publishes to every *land*,
> The *work* of an Almighty *hand*.
>
> Soon as the evening *shades* prevail,
> The *moon* takes up the wondrous *tale;*
> And nightly to the listening *earth*,
> Repeats the *story* of her *birth* ;
> While all the *stars* that round her burn,
> And all the *planets* in their *turn*,
> Confirm the *tidings* as they roll,
> And spread the *truth* from *pole* to *pole*.
>
> What though in solemn *silence* all,
> Move round this dark terrestrial *ball;*
> What though no real *voice* nor *sound*,
> Amid those radiant *orbs* be found ;
> In *Reason's ear* they all rejoice,
> And utter forth a glorious *voice*,
> Forever singing as they shine,
> " The HAND that made us is divine."

If we come closer to this *world*, and deal with *matters* of more local *interest*, we can find innumerable *subjects* of *conversation* and *correspondence:* The lightning *flash*, the thunder *peal*, the *storm* of *snow*, the *shower* of *rain*, the gentle *breeze*, the *gale* of *wind*, the hail-*drop* or the snow-*flake*. Besides these, we can speak of *continents* and *islands*, *oceans* and *seas*, *mountains* and *valleys*, *rivers* and *streams*, *forests* and *groves*, *fields* and *gardens*, *flowers* and *vegetables*, *cities* and *villages*, *empires* and *kingdoms*, *men* and *women*, *animals* and *birds*, *fishes* and *reptiles*, *insects* and *worms*. In fact, we can speak and write of every *thought* and *act* of every *member* of the human *race*, and of all higher *intelligences*. We can speak and write of every *thing* inhabiting the *land*, or living in the *waters;* of every *thing* found floating on the *ocean*, or buried in its *depths;* of every *thing* growing from the *soil*, or resting on its *bosom;* of every *thing* ornamenting our *persons*, or decorating our *houses;* of every *thing* poised in the *air*, or flashing through the *heavens*, created by DEITY, or invented by *man ;* existing anywhere from the *centre* of the *universe* to its remotest *verge*. The *name* of any *thing* and every *thing* is a NOUN.

COMMON AND PROPER NOUNS.

NOUNS are necessarily divided into *Common* and *Proper*.

A COMMON NOUN is a word that is *common* to *all its* *race* or *class*, and may be used to any one, without restriction or change ; as, *man*, *city*, *ocean*, *sea*, *river*, *mountain*, *ship*. Such words have no claim to capital letters, and they never should have them within the body of a sentence, no matter how great the temptation may be to act otherwise.

☞ A good illustration of the grammatical term "*Common*," as used in such phrases as *Common Nouns*, *Common Gender*, may be secured by calling to mind the

Central Park of New York, or the Boston Common. Within these beautiful inclosures the rich and poor can meet together, the millionaire and the beggar, the happy and the sad, the healthy and the invalid, the preacher and the politician, the stranger and the citizen. Ingress and egress without the slightest restriction are allowed; the inclosures are *common* to all. Hence the name given to the latter, the Boston " COMMON." This idea does not apply to individual properties; for it is well known that walls, palings, gates and locks, prevent their common use.

A PROPER NOUN is the individual name of *one* of any race or class; as, *John, Boston, Atlantic, Mediterranean, Hudson, Andes, Great Western.* These, and all other names individualizing any one from its fellows, are entitled to the capital letters, and must have them under every circumstance.

PERSON, GENDER, NUMBER, CASE.

NOUNS are said to be varied by Person, Gender, Number, and Case.

PERSON.

PERSON is that relation existing between the *speaker*, the *audience*, and the *subject of discourse*, or correspondence.

Thus, the speaker or writer, *while speaking or writing*, is *First Person*, and then and *then only* can make use of such words as *I, me, we, us.* The individual or audience, at *the time of being addressed*, is *Second Person*, and in such circumstances and in *those only*, the word

Thou, thee, ye or *you* is used. The person or persons, subject or subjects, spoken of, are in the *Third Person,* and in such cases the words, *he, him, she, her, they, them,* and *it,* are appropriate. Thus it may be perceived at once, that the only words which distinguish the different Persons, are Pronouns. But as *Nouns are merely names,* which can neither *speak* nor be *spoken to,* but only used in *speaking of,* it follows that THEY ARE ALWAYS IN THE THIRD PERSON, and *can never,* under any circumstance, be in the *First* or *Second* Person.

☞ This to some will be new doctrine, but it cannot be disproved. The "apposition" of the Noun with the Pronoun was nothing more than a convenient and deceptive invention, accepted by students in their ignorance, causing them much confusion and anxiety, without resulting in any benefit. I may confidently appeal to the best grammatical scholar in Christendom to point out to me *one solitary instance* in the English language, where an error can be created in *speaking* or *writing,* by recognizing and calling any Noun, a Noun in the Third Person, and *he cannot do it.* Where Nouns *are supposed* to be in the First or Second Person, it is the Pronoun, either expressed or understood, that is the subject of the Verb, and the Noun might as well be in parenthesis; as, I (Paul) have written it. If in this case the Noun Paul governed the Verb, or was the subject of it, the sentence would read thus; I, Paul, *has* written it, making grammatical nonsense.

GENDER.

GENDER has the same relation to Nouns that sex has to individuals. Nouns have four Genders : *Masculine, Feminine, Common,* and *Neuter.* There are only two Sexes : Male and Female.

The MASCULINE GENDER denotes the *Male Sex;* as, *Man, lion.*

The FEMININE GENDER denotes the *Female Sex;* as, *Woman, lioness.*

The COMMON GENDER denotes *either* Sex, and is expressed by a word common to both; as, *Child, parent, ancestor.*

The NEUTER GENDER denotes what is of *neither* Sex; as, *House, garden, piano.*

☞ It is seldom that an error is made in the use of the Gender. Few persons would say, John Henderson was *bridesmaid*, or Victoria is *king* of England.

NUMBER.

NUMBER is the distinction of *one* from *more.* There are two Numbers, the *Singular* and the *Plural.* The Singular denotes one; as, *Star, tree, flower.* The Plural denotes more than one; as, *Stars, trees, flowers.*

☞ The *Plural* is generally formed, as seen in the preceding examples, *by adding s to the Singular.* Nouns ending in *ss, sh, ch, x, o,* necessarily require *es;* as, Glasses, brushes, churches, foxes, heroes.

☞ *Nouns* ending in *y*, when a *consonant* precedes it, have *y* changed into *ies;* as, Lady, ladies; family, families. Nouns ending in *y* when a *vowel* precedes it retain the *y;* as, Attorney, attorneys; chimney, chimneys.

☞ *Remember particularly*, that whether the plural ends in *s*, an *es*, or an *ies*, the *last sound upon the ear* is that of "*s*"; hence euphony demands that the plural Verb should at all times *reject the additional s;* as, *Flowers grow*, not grows; *stars twinkle*, not twinkles.

☞ SINGULAR NOUNS coupled with *and* form a plural, and become an *equivalent to the plural ending in s,* requiring the same Verb; as, *John* and *Robert*—an equivalent to boys—play; *Mary* and *Lucy*—an equivalent to girls-laugh.

☞ The following *outlaws* never submit to rule:— *Man, men; woman, women; child, children; foot, feet; ox, oxen; tooth, teeth; goose, geese; mouse, mice; penny, pence.*

☞ SOME NOUNS are the *same* in both numbers; as, Sheep, deer, swine, hose, means, news, species, corps, apparatus.

☞ SOME NOUNS have *no Singular;* as, Embers, oats, tongs, scissors, vespers, ashes, clothes. Some have *no Plural;* as, Gold, mud, business, molasses, hay, flax, dust, pride, ambition.

☞ In pluralizing proper names, general usage sustains, the two *Miss Edmonsons,* the three *Miss Crosbys;* pedantic accuracy calls for, the two Misses Edmondson, the three Misses Crosby—the former is certainly the more preferable arrangement.

CASE.

CASE is the relation one Noun bears to another, or to a Verb, or Preposition. There are three Cases: the *Nominative, Possessive,* and *Objective.*

The *Nominative* simply names the *principal actor,* or agent, in the sentence; as, *Milton* wrote Paradise Lost; *Wars* impoverish a nation.

The *Possessive* implies possession; as, *Smith's* Astronomy; *Napoleon's* army.

The *Objective* denotes the object of a Verb or Preposition; as, Cicero expelled *Catiline;* The merchant lives within his *income.*

☞ The *Nominative* Case and the *Objective* are *always alike* in spelling and pronunciation; as, *God* created the universe; Saints worship *God*.

☞ In forming the Possessive Case, when the plural ends in *s*, the apostrophe only is added; as, The *Ladies'* Fair; the *Mechanics'* Institute.

☞ *Singular Nouns* ending in *s* must not be confused with those in the plural; hence instead of saying *Burns'* Poems, we should say *Burns's* Poems.

☞ When property is owned in common the *last term* only receives the Possessive sign; as, Hogg, Brown and *Taylor's* store.

☞ When individual ownership is expressed, *each* receives the sign; as, *Parker's* and *Wilson's* farm were sold yesterday. *Note*, we don't say *farms*, because one farm of each is meant; for if the Noun be made plural where it is expressed, it will also be plural where it is implied. Parker's and Wilson's *farms* would imply two or more of each; but Parker's and Wilson's farm only imply one belonging to each person. Perhaps, *Parker's farm and Wilson's* were sold yesterday, is a better arrangement for the singular: it is certainly more explicit.

☞ In forming the Possessive Case of Nouns that are the same in both numbers, the apostrophe is placed *before the s in the singular* number, *and after it in the plural;* as, Singular, Deer's; Plural, Deers'.

☞ *Of* is sometimes used to express the Possessive, and in harsh sentences is certainly preferable to the *'s*; as, The length of the day; The wisdom of Socrates. These phrases are certainly more elegant than, *The day's length*, or, *Socrates's wisdom*.

☞ The Preposition *of*, used to express the Possessive, leads occasionally to what is termed by some grammarians " Double Possessives;" as, This is a horse *of Kelley's*, namely, one of Kelley's horses; A speech *of President Grant's*, namely, one of President Grant's speeches. These Double Possessives are only allowable when the Noun is *distributive*, or one of many, as in the preceding examples.

NOMINATIVE, POSSESSIVE, OBJECTIVE.

> The *lightnings* flash along the *sky*,
> The *thunder* bursts and rolls on *high ;*
> *Jehovah's* voice methinks I hear
> Amid the *storm*,
> As riding on the *clouds* of *even*,
> He spreads his *glory* o'er the *heaven.*

ADJECTIVES.

ADJECTIVES imply character; or, an Adjective is a word added to a Noun, to give character to those objects which the Nouns represent; as, An *interesting* child; a *large* city; a *happy* home; a *pure* thought.

Every person and object in nature, from Deity on his throne, to the little pearly dew-drop trembling on the flower petal, possesses character, and the word that defines the character is an Adjective:—

> The *lofty* hill, the *humble* lawn,
> With *countless* beauties shine ;
> The *silent* grove, the *solemn* shade,
> Proclaim thy power *divine.*

COMPARISON.

COMPARISON is called into use when rivalry in character exists. There are *three Degrees* of Comparison :—the *Positive*, the *Comparative*, and the *Superlative*. The Positive expresses the *ordinary character* without comparison with any other ; as, Miss Ellis is a *tall* lady ; Boston is a *large* city. The Comparative is used when two characters are in *rivalry* with each other ; as, Miss Harding is *taller* than Miss Ellis ; New York is a *larger* city than Boston. The Superlative is used in the comparison of *three objects*, or more, and expresses the highest or lowest extreme of character ; as, Miss F. is the *tallest* lady in Boston ; Rhode Island is the *smallest* State in the Union.

☞ It will be seen from the preceding examples, that the Comparative of Adjectives is formed by adding *er* to the Positive; and the Superlative by adding *est ;* as Tall, tall*er*, tall*est*, small, small*er*, small*est*. Adjectives of *one* syllable should ever be compared in this way.

☞ ADJECTIVES of *three syllables*, and *more than three*, would offend the ear if compared by *er* and *est ;* as Courte-ous, courteous*er*, courteous*est ;* Ri-dic-u-lous, ridiculous*er*, ridiculous*est*. Hence such Adjectives *must* be compared by *more* and *most ;* as Courteous, *more* courteous, *most* courteous ; Ridiculous, *more* ridiculous, *most* ridiculous.

☞ Adjectives of *two* syllables, are like the Channel Islands in the English Sea, with France on one side, and England on the other ; the natives are found speaking both French and English. So it is with the two-syllable Adjectives, having on one side, those of one syllable compared by *er* and *est*, and on the other side, those

of three syllables compared by *more* and *most*, making
the two-syllable Adjectives susceptible of either form;
as, Po-lite, polit*er*, polit*est*; or, Polite, *more* polite, *most*
polite. In these, the speaker or writer can exercise his
own judgment and taste; for what he prefers is law.

☞ While the *two*-syllable Adjectives are susceptible
of *either* form of comparison, they do not admit of *both*
at one time; as, The *most* polit*est* lady; The *most* unkind*est* cut of all. These phrases would be correct if
written, The *politest* lady, the *unkindest* cut of all; or, The
most polite lady, the *most unkind* cut of all. No Adjective can stand the double dose of comparison at once.

☞ There is no grammatical error committed in using
several Adjectives before *one* Noun; as, Matilda is a *tall,
handsome, intelligent young* lady ; R. Thompson, Esq., is
an *able, practical,* and *experienced* lawyer.

☞ When two or more Adjectives requiring different
forms of comparison are placed before a Noun, the two
forms may be retained; as, It is the *neatest* and *most eligi-
ble* situation in the city ; A *sweeter* or *more amiable* lady
I have never seen. Good usage suggests an other form,
shorter it is true, but not quite so expressive ; namely, by
putting the grammatical sign of comparison before both ;
as, He is the *most* rich and enterprising man in the city;
I received the *most* shrewd and practical suggestions from
my Attorney. In these cases the smaller Adjective is
always placed before the larger ones.

☞ When two persons or objects are compared, and
two only, it is better to use the *Comparative* Degree,
than the Superlative ; as, James is *taller* than John, or
the taller of the two — *not* the tallest ; Mr. M. is *more
industrious* than Mr. B., or the more industrious of the
two — *not* the most industrious.

☞ There is no word in our language superlative in
itself, till it is made so by undergoing the ordinary process of comparison. A list of such words as some grammarians consider unsusceptible of comparison is made
out in most grammars, but this is waste labor; for the

best authors have swept those lists clean, and compared every word in them. Addison says, The eyes are the *most perfect* of our senses. Goldsmith says, And love is but an *emptier* name. The phrases, Most accurate, most sublime, most supreme, most conclusive, most permanent, &c., are all correct.

☞ The Numeral Adjectives, One, two, three, &c., First, second, third, &c., Single, double, &c., as well as the Adjectives, This, that, these, those, same, former, latter; each, every, either, neither; any, one, both, some, all, other, another, such, have no comparison. The latter are called "Pronominal Adjectives," because they are sometimes used as Pronouns; as, I paid a dollar for *this*. I would call them Adjectives when they are Adjectives, and Pronouns when they are Pronouns, and discourage the use of those compound names altogether.

☞ The following Adjectives are outlaws to rule, and will not be compared by the ordinary process of comparison; they have an arbitrary form of their own, and Princes and Presidents are powerless to alter it. *Good, bad, many, much*, and *little* will likely never submit to be compared regularly; as, Good, gooder, goodest; Bad, badder, baddest; much, mucher, muchest. Their own form they will take perhaps forever; as, Good, better, best; Bad, worse, worst; Much, more, most. The word "lesser," too, which according to Dr. Johnson is a barbarous corruption of less, is yet in frequent use by our most tasteful authors:—"It is the glowing style of a man who is negligent of *lesser* graces."—*Blair.* "These hills seem things of *lesser* dignity."—*Byron.* This word brought Webster to his knees much against his will: he says, "It is a corruption; but it is too well established to be discarded. Authors always write the *Lesser Asia*."

☞ A Noun frequently becomes an Adjective, when it is used to give character; as, A *gold* coin, a *silver* cup, the *morning* star. Adjectives of this kind are seldom compared:

Stone walls do not a prison make,
　Nor *iron* bars a cage ;
Minds innocent and quiet take,
　That for a hermitage.

A pebble in the streamlet scant,
　Has changed the course of many a river ;
A *dew* drop on the *baby* plant,
　Has warped the *giant* oak for ever.

PRONOUNS.

PRONOUNS are substitutes ; or, a Pronoun is a word that is used as a *substitute for a Noun;* as, Victoria is a happy queen : *she* reigns in the hearts of *her* people.

☞ Were there no Pronouns, our language would be burdened by the repetition of Nouns, as in the following sentence : When *Washington* had secured the independence of the United States, *Washington* retired to *Washington's* home, and gave *Washington's* attention to *Washington's* private business. Supply the Pronouns after the first Washington, and the sentence will read correctly : When Washington had secured the independence of the United States, *he* retired to *his* home, and gave *his* attention to *his* private business.

☞ Place a basket of fruit before a number of young friends, and the Pronouns will not be long in oblivion. Instead of the Noun apple, or apples, one says, I'll take *this;* an other *that;* a third, I prefer *these;* a fourth, *those;* a fifth, I want *none;* a sixth, I'll take an *other;* seventh, I don't care about *any;* eighth, here are two nice *ones,* I would like to have *both;* ninth, I cannot eat *such;* tenth, with a larger desire than any of his predecessors, I want *all;* eleventh, *What* has become of the apples? twelfth, *They* are *all* gone! *Who* has eaten *them?* These are legitimate Pronouns as used here; but if the Noun apple or apples were used, as, *this apple, those apples, this* and *those* would become Adjectives.

PRONOUNS are divided into *Personal, Relative, Demonstrative,* and *Distributive.*

PERSONAL PRONOUNS are used instead of the names of persons, hence their name *personal.* They are; *I, thou, he, she, it,* in the singular; and *We, you, they,* in the plural. In the order of cases they are: I, mine, me; We, ours, us. Thou, thine, thee; You, yours, you. He, his, him; They, theirs, them. She, hers, her; They, theirs, them. It, its, it; They, theirs, them.

☞ The Pronoun *thou* is never used at the present day, unless in addressing Deity, or amongst the Society of Friends. The Pronoun *you,* though once plural, is now used instead of *thou,* and has a singular signification when applied to an individual. It must always, however, retain its natural associations, and be accompanied with a *plural Verb;* as, You *are,* you *were,* you *have.* Webster's doctrine of a singular Verb accompanying it when used instead of thou, is very ridiculous ; for no ear could be tortured with such phrases as, You *is,* you *am,* you *art,* you *hast,* or you *was.*

☞ *We* in the plural is often used instead of *I* in the singular, especially by editors, authors, clergymen, reviewers, and monarchs. It lessens the individuality in the same manner as the Pronoun *you* does ; and like *you,* it must be followed with its *plural Verb* under every circumstance.

RELATIVE PRONOUNS are words which relate to Nouns or phrases going before them. They are *Who, which,* and *that.* Who is applied to persons, or the higher intelligences generally; as, God *who* created the universe is of infinite power; The man *who* possesses wealth should be generous; The lady *who* wrote that poem possesses much sweetness of disposition; The boy *who* honors his parents will be respected; The girl *who* was crowned "queen" by her classmates, was delighted with the honor.

☞ *Which* is applied to animals and inanimate objects; as, The elephant *which* escaped from his keeper has been captured; The rose *which* she plucked has faded. Which is sometimes elegantly omitted:

> I hear a voice—thou canst not hear,
> Which says thou must not stay;
> I see a hand—thou canst not see,
> Which beckons me away.

☞ THAT is used when it would be improper to use either *who* or *which,* or when the repetition of either *becomes offensive;* as, The Sailor and boat *that* passed the Light House were never heard from; (Here *which* would be wrong because *sailor requires* WHO; and *who* would be wrong because *boat requires* WHICH: the difficulty is got over by using *that.*) It was Columbus *that* discovered America; The watch *that* I found I returned to its owner.

☞ The Noun or phrase to which the relative belongs, is called the *Antecedent,* and the Relative is dependent upon it for its *Person, Gender,* and *Number.* In the last example above, "that" is in the *third* Person, *neuter* Gender, and *singular* Number, because "Watch," its antecedent, is in the *third* Person, *neuter* Gender, *singular* Number.

☞ The COMPOUND RELATIVES include both the Antecedent and the Relative; as, *Whoever* said so spoke truly; that is, The *man who* said so spoke truly. The

Compound Relatives are, Whoever, whosoever, whomso-
ever; whichever, whichsoever; what, whatever, and
whatsoever.

☞ When the relative has lost its antecedent, it finds it
immediately, by changing itself into an Interrogative; as
Who wrote the Illiad, and was called the Prince of Poets?
Answer: Homer.   In this way some of the Relatives
become what grammarians call "Interrogative Pronouns."

☞ *Who* and *Which*, as Relatives and as Interrogatives, are thus declined in the order of their cases: Singular and Plural, *Who, whose, whom; Which, whose,
which.   What* has no variation.   *That* has *whose* in the
Possessive, but has no objective.   *Whoever* and *whosoever*
are declined like *who.*

☞ *Whose*, as the true Possessive of *which*, is sanc-
tioned by the best classical authority: "A triangle, one of
whose sides is perpendicular to another."—*Brougham;*
"Cedar groves *whose* gigantic branches threw a refreshing
coolness over the verdure."—*Prescott.*

DEMONSTRATIVE PRONOUNS specify particularly what
objects or words are meant.   The Demonstratives are,
This, that, these, those, former, and *latter.*

☞ When two objects that may be seen are con-
trasted, *this* refers to the one *near the speaker*, and *that* to
the one further away; as, *This*—referring to the object
near—cost four dollars ; *that* cost two.

☞ When *words* passing from the lips are contrasted,
this refers to the one last spoken, and *that* to the first,
because it is further away; as, The *rose* and *lily* are
emblematical; *this* of purity, *that* of honesty.

> *Self-love*, the spring of motion guides the soul ;
> Reason's comparing *balance* rules the whole :
> Man but for *this*, no motion could attend,
> And but for *that*, were active to no end.

☞ When *objects* in the plural, that may be seen, are
contrasted, *these* refers to the ones near the speaker, and

those to the ones further away; as, *These*—flowers near at hand—emit delicious perfume, *those* are faded and worthless.

☞ When *words* in the plural are contrasted, *these* refers to the one last spoken, and *those* to the first; as, It is better to fall among *vultures* than *flatterers; those* devour the dead only, *these* the living.

> Farewell my *friends!* Farewell my *foes!*
> My peace with *these,* my love to *those.—Burns.*

☞ *Former* and *latter* have a similar use; as, *Body and soul* must part; the *latter* wings its way to its Almighty source, the *former* drops into the dark and silent grave.

DISTRIBUTIVE PRONOUNS are those which refer to a number of objects taken separately. They are *Each, every, either, neither.* Distributive Pronouns are always used in the *Singular Number* and in the *Third Person,* even when they relate to the persons speaking, the persons addressed, as well as to the persons spoken of; as, Each of *us* had more than *he* wanted; Each of *you* had more than *he* wanted; Each of *them* had more than *he* wanted.

☞ *Every* was once in good standing as a Pronoun, but as it cannot be now used without its Noun it is a mere Adjective. We can say, each received a prize; but we cannot say, every received a prize: every requires its Noun after it to make sense; as, Every *student* received a prize for his good behavior; Every *tempest* and every *dew-drop* has its mission;

> Every *tongue* and every *eye*
> *Does* homage to the passer-by.

☞ *Each* denotes *two* or *more* objects; *Every* denotes *more than two; Either* and *Neither* refer to *two only* and never more. If a greater number than two be named, where it might appear that Either or Neither could be used, adopt the terms *any one,* or *not one* as the case may be ; as, Three or more houses were searched for stolen property, and none was found in *any one* of them; Three or more prisoners were tried yesterday, and *not one* of them was found guilty.

☞ As there is no *Pronoun of the* COMMON GENDER in the English language, speakers and writers are continually under the necessity of using such terms as, he or she, his or hers, him or her, in speaking or writing of a mixed company, to avoid using the plural pronoun they, their, theirs, or them, which would be quite ungrammatical in this connection. Nothing is more offensive to an educated ear than to hear a person say, Every one should dress according to *their* own taste and fancy; it should be, "according to *his* or *her* own taste and fancy."

☞ Either and Neither, as *Pronouns*, must be carefully distinguished from Either and Neither as *Adjectives*, or *Conjunctions*. When *Pronouns*, they are used *instead of*, not *along with*, their Nouns; as, Either of the roads is good ; Neither of the offices is filled. When *Adjectives*, they are used *with their Nouns ;* as, You can take *either* road you please ; *Neither office* will suit the candidate. When *Conjunctions*, they may connect *not only two Nouns, but several ;* as, I am satisfied that *either* John, or William, or Edward, or Thomas, broke the looking-glass ; For I am persuaded that *neither* death, nor life, nor angels, nor principalities, nor things present, nor things to come, nor hight, nor depth, nor any other creature shall be able to separate us from the love of God.

VERBS.

VERBS imply action; or, a Verb is a word that expresses something of its Noun or nominative; as, Time *flies*, stars *twinkle;* monarchs *rule*, the sun *shines*. Verbs are of three kinds : Transitive, Passive, and Neuter.

TRANSITIVE Verbs express action passing over from an actor to an object; as, Antony *beheaded* Cicero; Milton *wrote* Paradise Lost.

☞ The action represented by the Transitive Verb passes like the arrow from the bow of the archer to its victim beyond, and strikes with unerring certainty. Should the arrow droop in its flight and fail to strike, no Transitive Verb in that particular instance existed.

☞ While every school and college in America and Great Britain teaches that the Transitive Verbs of our language govern Thirty thousand Nouns and sixty Pronouns ; and every teacher and student believes that in every word lies a possible error, it should form an interesting fact in the history of Grammar, to learn that the Transitive Verbs govern or control only SEVEN WORDS altogether : *Me, thee, him, her, us, them,* and *whom.* When these words are correctly used in speaking and writing, there is not an other word in the English language in which an error can take place, under the influence of the Transitive Verbs for ever !

☞ To insure correctness in this particular, the necessary effort will not occupy more than *five* or *ten minutes* labor, while as many *years* fail to establish or secure equal certainty, as the Science is now taught throughout the world. All that has to be done is to make use of any Transitive Verb required in connection with those seven words named, and familiarize the tongue with them : as,

> The President invited *me*.
> The President invited *thee*.
> The President invited *him*.
> The President invited *her*.
> The President invited *us*.
> The President invited *them*.
> The President invited *whom*.

PASSIVE VERBS are those which represent the receiving or suffering of the action of an other; as, Cicero *was beheaded* by Antony; Moscow *was taken* by Napoleon.

☞ In the formation of Passive Verbs, they are found to be the mere reverse of the Transitive; thus, Brutus *stabbed* Cæsar is Transitive; and Cæsar *was stabbed* by Brutus, is Passive.

NEUTER VERBS, very appropriately called by some grammarians *Intransitive*, represent a state of existence, or action, confined to the actor; as, Flowers *grow*: The sentinel *sleeps*; The river Jordan *flows* into the Dead Sea. The Neuter Verb *Be*, or some part of it, is *at all times* used as an *auxilliary* in the formation of the Passive : as, The criminal will *be* pardoned ; The oak *was* shattered by lightning : The cities *were* destroyed by an earthquake.

MOOD or Mode means manner; and, grammatically, shows the manner in which the Verb states something of its Nominative. Verbs have four Moods : The *Indicative, Potential, Subjunctive,* and *Imperative.*

The *Indicative* asserts an *actual occurrence*, or living truth; as, Prince Arthur *visited* the United States; Galileo *invented* the telescope;

> That very law that moulds a tear,
> And bids it trickle from its source;
> That law *preserves* the earth a sphere,
> And *guides* the planets in their course.

☞ The facts asserted by the Indicative may have reference to any time, past, present, or future; as, Nero *burned* Rome; Victoria *reigns* in England; Henry W. Beecher *will preach* in Washington next Sunday.

☞ The Indicative asks questions also; as, Did Nero burn Rome? Does Victoria reign in England? Will Henry W. Beecher preach in Washington next Sunday?

The *Potential* implies the power to do, or asserts the mere possibility of an action; as, The President *can pardon* political prisoners; Charles Dickens *may repeat* his visit to America.

> Potential means the having power or will;
> As, If you *would* improve, you *should* be still.—*Tobitt.*

☞ The Potential, like the Indicative, asks questions; and these are the only Moods which can be changed into Interrogatives:

> *Can* storied urn or animated bust,
> Back to its mansion call the fleeting breath?
> *Can* Honor's voice provoke the silent dust,
> Or flattery soothe the dull, cold ear of death?

The *Subjunctive* represents an action depending on a future uncertainty; as, If thy brother *trespass* against thee, rebuke him; and, if he *repent*, forgive him.

☞ It is the *future uncertainty* in the mind of the speaker, and *not* the Conjunction "If," that calls particularly for the Subjunctive Mood: as, If it *rain* to-morrow I cannot go to Charlestown. *If* is frequently used in the Indicative, expressing an admitted fact; as, If he *has* money he keeps it.

☞ Grammarians have ever found the Subjunctive Mood a puzzle and a source of much annoyance; hence the desire so visibly manifested to bring it into disuse. To me it is one of the special beauties of the English language, giving the speaker the power of expressing all future uncertainties, in distinct and direct contrast with the certainties of the Indicative. The following rule will, I hope, be sufficiently explicit, to make it practically useful under every circumstance:—Drop the final s from the Present Indicative:—

INDICATIVE.	SUBJUNCTIVE.
He pays.	If he pay.
He pardons.	If he pardon.
He repents.	If he repent.
He refuses.	If he refuse.
He persecutes.	If he persecute.

☞ To this simple rule there are only two exceptions in the language, namely the two radical verbs Have and Be. When these are added, all will be complete:—Indic. He *is;* Sub. *If* he *be.* Indic. He *has;* Sub. If he *have.* Indic. He *was;* Sub. If he *were,* or, were he.

☞ The distinctive characteristic of the Subjunctive Mood is, that it *never changes its form* like the Indicative. As soon as it is found for one person, it is had for every person, whether in the Singular Number or in the Plural, for ever:—

INDICATIVE.		SUBJUNCTIVE.	
I work.	We work.	If I *work.*	If we *work.*
Thou workest.	You work.	If thou *work.*	If you *work.*
He works.	They work.	If he *work.*	If they *work.*
I pardon.	We pardon.	If I *pardon.*	If we *pardon.*
Thou pardonest.	You pardon.	If thou *pardon.*	If you *pardon.*
He pardons.	They pardon.	If he *pardon.*	If they *pardon.*
I am.	We are.	If I *be.*	If we *be.*
Thou art.	You are.	If thou *be.*	If you *be.*
He is.	They are.	If he *be.*	If they *be.*
I have.	We have.	If I *have.*	If we *have.*
Thou hast.	You have.	If thou *have.*	If you *have.*
He has.	They have.	If he *have.*	If they *have.*

The IMPERATIVE is that Mood or form of the Verb by which we urge our claims and wishes upon others. First, upon our inferiors, by *command;* as, Go! Second, upon our equals, by *counsel;* as, Honor thy father and thy mother. Third, upon our superiors, by *supplication;* as, Give us this day our daily bread.

COUNSEL.

Deal with another as you'd have
Another deal with you ;
What you're unwilling to receive,
Be sure you never do.

SUPPLICATION.

Thou Being,
All seeing,
O, hear my fervent prayer;
Still take her,
And make her,
Thy most peculiar care!

TENSE is the distinction of time. The great ocean of time, with its restless surface ever in motion, is spread out before us, and lies at our feet. There are waves ever present, lashing the shore where we stand; waves ever receding, and waves ever approaching, making the three grand divisions of time, the PRESENT, PAST and FUTURE. These are again very appropriately sub-divided into, the *Present,* and *Present Perfect;* the *Past,* and *Past Perfect;* and the *Future,* and *Future Perfect.*

The PRESENT TENSE expresses what *now exists,* or is taking place; as, The sun *shines;* The flowers *are* growing.

☞ The PRESENT TENSE expresses all periods of time embracing the *present moment;* as, This hour, this day, this year, this century.

☞ The PRESENT TENSE is used to express all great truths; as, Vice *produces* misery; Virtue *elevates* the human race.

☞ The PRESENT TENSE is used to express all habits and customs; as, Edward *smokes;* Emily *dresses* neatly; The sun *rises* every morning and *sets* every evening.

☞ The PRESENT TENSE is used in animated narration to express past events, creating an interest in the speaker's mind, so that the events seem to be passing before him; as, Cæsar *leaves* Gaul, *crosses* the Rubicon, and *enters* Rome in triumph.

> What sounds upon the midnight wind
> *Approach* so rapidly behind?
> It *is*, it *is*, the tramp of steeds;
> Matilda *hears* the sound, she *speeds*,
> *Seizes* upon the leader's rein.

The PRESENT PERFECT Tense is used to represent past events as perfectly finished in present time; as, We *have completed* the task; My father *has purchased* the estate.

☞ This Tense is used to express past events whose effects remain to the present; as, Milton *has written* some noble works; Cicero *has written* orations. We cannot say, Cicero has written poems, because they have ceased to exist; in this instance we would say, Cicero *wrote* poems.

This Tense is very comprehensive, and grasps all past time, from the Creation to the present. It matters not how long ago the action may have been performed, the phraseology of the Present Perfect may be used, so long as the *time* of the action *is not named;* as, God has created the heavens.

☞ When the time of the event is mentioned, however near it may be to the present, the phraseology must be changed into that of the Past Tense; as, I *have seen* the Prince a moment ago; should be, I *saw* the Prince a moment ago.

The use of this Tense is so delicately beautiful in its application to language, that it cannot be used, if the slightest hint is made to any point of past time; as, He has been *formerly* subject to fits of insanity; should be, He *was* formerly subject to fits of insanity.

The PAST TENSE is used to express past events; as, David *loved* Jonathan; The Empress Eugenia *was* present at the opening of the Suez Canal.

☞ This Tense like the Present sometimes denotes custom ; as,

> Thirty steeds, both fleet and wight,
> *Stood* saddled in stable day and night,
> A hundred more *fed* free in stall ;
> Such was the custom in Bransome hall.

The PAST PERFECT Tense is used to express actions or events completely finished in past time, before other actions or events took place ; as, The ship *had sailed* before he reached Glasgow ; The cars *had started* when he arrived at the station.

In order to use this Tense correctly, allow the two actions or events to pass before the imagination, and use *had* to the *first* one, as in the preceding examples.

The FUTURE Tense represents future actions ; as, I *will see* you again, and your heart *shall* rejoice.

This Tense may foretell a future custom ; as, The wolf *shall dwell* with the lamb ; The lion *shall eat* straw like the ox.

The FUTURE PERFECT is used to represent finished actions in future time ; as, The fortress when finished *will have cost* a million.

☞ This Tense represents actions or events limited to a certain point of time in the future, forming as it were a barrier thrown up in the way, past which the performance of the action cannot pass. The action thus arrested is forced to be fully completed, before the limiting point of time is reached ; as, The debt *will have been paid* before the first of June next ; The mansion *will have been completed* before New Year's day.

WILL AND SHALL.

These two words have very different meaning, as may be seen from the following examples : I *will* be drowned and nobody *shall* save me ; I *shall* be drowned and nobody *will* save me.

☞ WILL. When a person *resolves for himself*, he uses *will;* as, I *will* write to Washington to-day.

☞ SHALL. When a person *resolves for another*, he uses *shall*, and the use of this word implies an authority in the speaker to enforce the act if necessary : as, You *shall* pay that bill to-morrow ; he *shall* leave the establishment for his impertinence.

☞ WILL. When a person foretells or simply PRE-DICTS *for another*, he uses *will;* as, He *will* remove to Philadelphia in the Spring.

☞ SHALL. When a person foretells or simply PRE-DICTS *for himself*, he uses *shall;* as, I *shall* see my father this afternoon. Brightland writes :

> In the FIRST PERSON simply *shall foretells*,
> In *will* a THREAT or else a PROMISE dwells.
> *Shall*, in the SECOND and the THIRD, does *threat ;*
> *Will*, simply, then, *foretells* the future feat.

REGULAR AND IRREGULAR VERBS.

The English language is supposed to contain about 8000 Verbs, of which upwards of 7800 are *Regular*. These form their *Past* tense and *Present Perfect*, by a uniform process of adding *d* or *ed* to the Present; as, I love, I loved, I have loved; I preach, I preached, I have preached. Those Verbs which do not form their *Past* tense and *Present Perfect* by undergoing a similar process are called *Irregular;* as, I see, I saw, I have seen; He knows, he knew, he has known.

☞ The IRREGULAR VERBS are gradually and steadily growing fewer and fewer every day ; and the time will probably come when they can be numbered by the dozen or the score, instead of by the hundred as they are to-day. Watch the infant boy as he first lisps our language, catching up its spirit and its tendency, shouting, I *seed* him do it; I *knowed* he'd break my pencil; the bee *stinged* me. Of course the educated ear very properly rejects these offensive intrusions, and more particularly as they are reëchoed from the lips of older persons ; but, judging from the past, and noting the steadily increasing pressure of the Regular Verbs upon the lessening minority, the fate of the Irregular Verbs is certain.

Once it was quite correct to say, She *holp* her friend ; he *clomb* the fence ; it *snew* yesterday ; he *wrought* a week. Now we say, She *helped* her friend ; he *climbed* the fence ; it *snowed* yesterday ; he *worked* a week. So words change, and the *knew* of the present century, may, in the distant future become as ridiculous to the ear, as the *clomb* or *snew* of our ancestors is to us to-day. Milton wrote :

So *clomb* the first grand thief into God's fold ;
So since into his church lewd hirelings climb.

☞ While the Irregular Verbs exist, the true scholar is familiar with every one of them and uses it properly. In all our Text-books of Grammar they stand in three columns, headed and arranged as follows :

IRREGULAR VERBS.

Present.	Past.	Past Participle.
Am,	Was,	Been,
Arise,	Arose,	Arisen, &c.

The student, instead of reciting these as school-boys generally do, Present *Am*, Past *was*, Past Participle *been*, should place a Pronoun before each, and slowly repeat it thus : I am, I was, I have been ; I arise, I arose, I have arisen ; remembering particularly that the Past Participle *must ever* have an auxiliary before it, as above.

☞ I see no use in grammarians retaining in their list of Irregular Verbs as they do, those which are regular. If regular, let them be used as such ; and in this way the long list of Irregular Verbs will be much reduced, and

the science of the English tongue much simplified.
Lord Kames, in his Elements of Criticism, highly eulo-
gises Dean Swift, for rejecting, in his time, many of those
"ugly" contractions. So, in this day, the person who
by counsel or example, will assist in the good work of
establishing a uniformity in our language by lessening
the number of irregular contractions, and speaking and
writing those of them as regular which are regular, will
equally deserve well of the present and future generations.

☞ I have carefully selected the following Verbs
marked *R*, from the Irregular Verbs of the Text-books.
They are recognized by all grammarians as Regular; and
as such, the sooner they are brought into universal usage
the better: Acquit, awake; Bereave, bless, blow, burn
burst; Catch, clothe, creep, crow, curse; Dare, dive,
dream, dress, dwell; Gild, gird; Heat, heave, hew;
Kneel, knit; Lean, leap, learn, light; Mean, mow;
Pass, pen, plead, prove; Quit; Roast; Saw, seethe,
shape, shave, shear, shine, show, smell, sow, spell, spoil,
stave, stay, swell; Thrive, throw; Wake, wax, wed, weep,
whet, work. By this arrangement, the Irregular Verbs
of the language will be reduced to about a hundred.

AUXILIARY VERBS are those which assist others; as,
He *was* invited; and they can be only used *before* Past
Participles under any circumstance; as, He *had seen;*
He *has won;* We *have written.*

DEFECTIVE VERBS are those which want some of their
principal parts; as,

Present.	*Past.*	*Past Participle.*
Can	Could	Wanting
May	Might	—
Must	Must	—
Ought	Ought	—
Shall	Should	—
Will	Would	—
Quoth	Quoth	—

☞ From the preceding list it will be visible that the
Defective Verbs have no Participle; and hence there is

not one word of them before which an Auxiliary can be placed. The impropriety then of saying, I *had* ought, I *hadn't* ought, is understood; and it is just as ridiculous as if the Auxiliary had been placed before any other Defective Verb in the list; as, He *had* can; He *had* must; He *had* quoth; He *had* ought. Take away the Auxiliary *had*, and the expressions will be correct; as, He *can* do so; He *must* do so; He *ought* to do so.

"S."

To secure a simple form of agreement between the Noun and Verb, is an object of much anxiety to many, and it should be one of ardent aspiration to all, and to extemporaneous speakers particularly. As social conversation and public addresses are so generally conducted in the Third Person and Present Tense, the speaker should remember that the Plural of Nouns is formed by adding an *s* to the singular, and the Plural of Verbs by dropping the *s* from the singular; consequently in all Syntactical agreement, there is only one *s* between the two.

Suppose then this *s* suspended between the Noun and the Verb, to be at liberty to vibrate between them, and pass from one to the other, a most interesting and singular simplicity of agreement is secured in every vibration:

NOUN.   VERB.

APPLE   FLOWER   JEWEL   S   GLITTER   BLOSSOM   RIPEN

When the *s* vibrates to the side of the Noun and attaches itself to it, we have the Verb and Noun Plural; and when the *s* vibrates to the side of the Verb and attaches itself to it, we have the Verb and Noun Singular:

PLURAL.	SINGULAR.
The apples ripen.	The apple ripens.
The flowers blossom.	The flower blossoms.
The jewels glitter.	The jewel glitters.

☞ An equivalent to the Noun in the Plural requires the same form of Verb; as, The *boys read* correctly. = *John* and *Thomas read* correctly. The *girls sing* sweetly. = *Ellen* and *Lucy sing* sweetly. *Empires sustain* large standing armies. = *France* and *Russia sustain* large standing armies.

☞ The only exceptions to the preceding "*s*" arrangement are found in the three words, *Is, was*, and *has*. It does not require much effort to remember, that whenever these words are used, either as Auxiliaries or Principal Verbs, they are changed into *are, were*, and *have* in the plural. Hence we say, The *bird is* singing, the *birds are* singing; The *doctor was* called, the *doctors were* called; The *hour has* passed pleasantly, the *hours have* passed pleasantly.

PARTICIPLES are words that *participate* in the nature of a Noun, the nature of an Adjective, and the nature of a Verb. They are manufactured from the Radical Verb, always found in the Present Infinitive; as, To *wonder*. Add *ing* to wonder, and the Present Participle is secured; as, *Wondering*. Remove the *ing*, and add *ed*, and the Past Participle is secured; as, *Wondered*. Place *having* before the Past Participle, and the Perfect Participle is secured; as, *Having wondered*. In this way the Participles may be secured from every Regular Verb in the language.

☞ The difference between the Verb and the Participle is this :- the Verb asserts; as, He *betrayed* his friend. The Participle never asserts; as, *Betrayed*, he is unhappy.

☞ Participles *influence* and *govern* words, in the same manner as the Verbs from which they emanated.

ADVERBS.

ADVERBS give character to action; or, an **Adverb** is a word that qualifies a Verb, an Adjective, or another Adverb; as, Peter wept *bitterly;* Harriet is *exceedingly* clever; John speaks *very* distinctly. The Adverbs promote brevity, and add much to the beauty of the language, making it concise and elegant:

> So *still* he sat as those who wait,
> Till judgment speak the doom of fate!

☞ The multifarious and metaphysical divisions of the Adverb beyond those of *manner, time,* and *place* may form an exceedingly pleasant pastime to the writer of a Text-book, for school exercises; and they certainly afford a rich opportunity of bewildering the student in his perplexing pilgrimage of parsing and analyzing; but they are of no practical value to the speaker, for his ignorance of them will never cause an error.

☞ In the use of the Adverb it is only necessary to know three things: First, that an Adverb *is* really *required;* Second, to know *how* to secure it; and Third, to know *where* to put it. An Adverb is required when the speaker wishes to give character to action; as, The canary sings (in what manner?) sweetly. The lady dances (in what manner?) gracefully. These Adverbs were secured by adding *ly* to the two Adjectives Sweet and Graceful, making them *sweetly*, *gracefully*. In this manner four-fifths of the Adverbs of the language may be manufactured by simply adding *ly* to the Adjective. Hence we have polite*ly*, imprudent*ly*, quiet*ly*, attentive*ly*, handsome*ly*, religious*ly*, temperate*ly*, sufficient*ly*, ridiculous*ly*, particular*ly*, intelligent*ly*, and more than a thousand others.

☞ To place the Adverb, the best general rule is,—In Transitive Verbs place the Adverb after the object reached; as, John struck Thomas *rashly*; the lightning killed the man *instantly*. In Passive Verbs place the Adverb between the Auxiliary and the Verb; as, Thomas was *rashly* struck; The man was *instantly* killed. In Neuter Verbs place the Adverb immediately after the Verb; as, The wind blows *furiously*; The flowers grow *rapidly*.

☞ Whenever the complying with this rule would alter the sense or weaken it, it should be promptly suspended, and the Adverb located where the speaker's meaning would be more correctly expressed.

☞ When Adverbs qualify Adjectives or other Adverbs, the qualifying word is always placed before them; as, It is a *particularly* interesting story; They conducted themselves *very* improperly.

☞ An *Adjective*, not an Adverb, should always follow a Neuter Verb when it qualifies the Noun preceding it and not the Verb itself; as, The fields look *green*; Lizzie appears *contented* and happy: The wind blows *fresh*; Prince Arthur looked *splendid*.

☞ Two negatives contradicting each other ought to be carefully avoided; as, Death *never* spared *no* one; should be, Death *never* spared *any* one.

PREPOSITIONS.

PREPOSITIONS imply *position;* or a Preposition is a word that shows the relative position of two or more objects to one another; as, The rose blooms *in* the garden ; The river flows *between* the hills; The eagle soars *above* the mountain summits; My sister stands *behind* me.

☞ Take any two articles, such as a tumbler and a goblet, and change their position in reference to each other; in this way the most of the Prepositions may be manufactured to the eye; as, Above, over, on, in, within, without, out of, before, behind, across, around, down, near, up, from, toward, to, against, under, underneath, &c. The few remaining ones have reference more to words or ideas than to objects.

☞ The Preposition's governing power is limited to the SEVEN WORDS governed by the Transitive Verbs, namely: *Me, thee, him, her, us, them,* and *whom.*

☞ When a Preposition stands before a single Pronoun, there is seldom an error made; as, Before *me* — no one would say, before *I;* but when the Preposition is followed by *two* Pronouns, nothing but the grammatical knowledge of the proper word to be used will save the speaker from erring. How often do we hear from professedly educated persons, Between *you* and *I;* between

you and *she!* Now these phrases are as grammatically
wrong as, Over *I*, over *she;* but the ear is deceived by
the close association, of *you* with these words, and the
error is in a measure concealed by it. The Pronoun
YOU is a dangerous companion for any other Pronoun to
be connected with, and will assuredly lead to error if not
carefully watched and guarded against.

☞ Prepositions have a beautiful use in the language
not recognized by grammarians. To understand this, it
must be remembered that all Transitive Verbs reach
objects ; the Passive and Neuter of themselves never do.
These, like the drooping arrow of the archer, caught in
its falling by a friendly hand and sped on to its mark,
receive an impetus from the Prepositions, forming a com-
bination equal to a Transitive Verb ; as, Saturn's ring
was seen through the telescope; The river *flows into* the
ocean.

ACTOR.   *Transitive Verb, or action.*   OBJECT.
...

                Passive.
....

                Neuter.
....

ACTOR.   *Transitive Verb, or action.*   OBJECT.
...

                Passive, with Preposition.
...

                Neuter, with Preposition.
...

☞ This feature in the use of the Prepositions, suggests an interesting thought, either morally or philosophi-
cally considered, that ALL VERBS ARE TRANSITIVE, or
may be so; having one COMMON DESTINY, namely, to
reach and influence objects beyond.

☞ The Preposition should be placed immediately before the Relative it governs; as, *With whom* do you associate? Not, *Who* do you associate *with?*

☞ SINCE is very frequently and improperly confused with AGO; as, He called four days since. It ought to be remembered that *since* should be only used in measuring time from the past towards the present, and *ago*, in measuring from the present towards the past; as, I have not seen him *since* Christmas; He called a week *ago*.

☞ IN is very improperly used for INTO to express entrance; as, Robert went *in* the Common; should be, went *into* the Common. It should be remembered that being outside the enclosure he would first have to go TO the boundary line, and then IN, before an entrance could be accomplished; hence the proper use of the beautiful compound word *into*.

☞ BETWEEN is frequently and improperly used for *among;* as, I divided the money *between* the four boys; should be, *among* the four boys. *Between* has reference to TWO *only*, and *among* has reference to any greater number *than two;* as, He sat *between* his two sisters; He spent the winter *among* his country relatives.

CONJUNCTIONS.

CONJUNCTIONS unite; or, a Conjunction is a word that connects words or sentences together; as, Milton *and* Shakspeare were poets; Washington was a true patriot, *therefore* his country reveres his memory. The words generally used as Conjunctions are: Also, and, as well as, but, yet, nevertheless, nor, notwithstanding, or, neither, if, though, unless, for, since, lest, than, because, inasmuch.

☞ CONJUNCTIONS are used to connect together the scattered shreds of language and fit them to convey a connected train of thought. Were there no Conjunctions the act of speaking or writing would be tedious and laborious, as every object or action would then have to be spoken of separately. Mott says:—

> The current is often evinced by the straws,
>   And the course of the wind by the flight of a feather;
> So a speaker is known by his *ands* and his *ors*,
>   Those stitches that fasten his patchwork together.

The following sentence will illustrate the poet's idea of stitching:—Italy teems with recollections of every kind; for courage, *and* wisdom, *and* power, *and* arts, *and* science, *and* beauty, *and* music, *and* desolation, have all made it their dwelling place.

☞ Conjunctions couple the same Cases of Nouns or Pronouns, for a similar reason, that two chained balls must fly in *one direction* from the mouth of the cannon. Being hinged together by the Conjunction, the Nouns or Pronouns must represent ACTION in concert; POSSESSION in concert, or SUFFERING in concert; as, *James* and *Edward* went to New York; *Susan's*, as well as *Matilda's*, boots, were purchased on Broadway; George Peabody's donations benefited *England* and *America*.

☞ Conjunctions couple the same Moods and Tenses of Verbs; as, Napoleon FOUND Moscow in flames *and* instantly ORDERED his troops to extinguish them.

☞ Sometimes Conjunctions connect different Moods and Tenses, but in such cases euphony and perspicuity require the Nominative to be repeated; as, He came and *he* would not stay; The flowers are now covered beneath the Winter's snow, but when Spring shall arrive, *they* will bud forth and blossom, delighting the senses with their beauty and fragrance.

☞ CORRELATIVE CONJUNCTIONS are composed of two corresponding words; when the first of these is used, the other should be used also. Examples:—

NEITHER—NOR.

The Hectar, wrapped in everlasting sleep,
Shall *neither* hear thee cry, *nor* see thee weep.

EITHER—OR.

I will *either* mail the letter, *or* forward it by Express.

THOUGH—YET.

Though deep *yet* clear; *though* gentle *yet* not dull.

SO—THAT.

He was *so* fatigued *that* he could hardly move.

OTHER, and the *Comparative* Degree, THAN.

No *other than* she; He is *richer than* his brother.

SAME—AS.

Your hat is of the *same* style *as* mine.

NOT ONLY—BUT ALSO.

He was *not only* prudent *but also* industrious.

AS—SO.

As down in the sunless retreats of the ocean,
Sweet flowerets are springing, no mortal can see ;
So deep in my bosom, the prayer of devotion,
Unheard by the world, rises silent to thee.

INTERJECTIONS.

INTERJECTIONS express emotion ; or, an Interjection is a word caused by some sudden and exciting sensation of the mind ; as, *Hark!* the bell tolls. *Oh!* make her a grave where the sunbeams rest. *See!* the eclipse is now complete.

☞ Interjections are those words which escape the lips when the mind becomes full to overflowing of uncontrollable emotion ; and such words, although having no grammatical connection, are particularly expressive and give soul to language. Besides the ordinary Interjections, which in many cases are mere sounds, any other part of speech may become an Interjection; as, Nonsense! Shocking! Wonderful! Silence! Welcome!

O, AND' OH.

O, is used in direct address; as, O virtue! O sister! and it should always be suggestive of something pleasant, joyful and interesting; as, O, the sunny days of childhood! Oh! is used to express emotions of pain, sorrow, trouble, or suffering of some kind, requiring the exclamation point next it; and it may or may not, as the writer wishes, have another at the end of the sentence; as, Oh! what untold sorrows were created by the late war!

> *Oh!* had your fate been joined to mine,
> As once this pledge appeared the token;
> These follies had not then been mine,
> My early vows had not been broken.—*Byron.*

CAPITAL LETTERS.

The first word of every distinct sentence should begin with a capital letter; as, *Simple* pleasures give the highest enjoyment. The first word of every line in Poetry should begin with a capital; as,

Of heaven if thou would'st reach a gleam,
On humblest object fix thy eyes;
So travelers, in a picturing stream,
Look down, indeed, but see the skies.

☞ The following words always require capital letters: Proper Nouns and titles of honor; as, *Ottawa; Sir* Walter Scott; *Judge* Wilkinson. Adjectives derived from names of places; as, American, Spanish, Prussian. The first word of a direct quotation when it forms a complete sentence; as, Virgil says, "Labor conquers all." The Pronoun I, and the Interjection O. The names of the days of the week; as, Sunday, Monday. The names of the months of the year; as, January, February, March. Every appellation of Deity; as, God, Almighty, Jehovah. Every Noun and principal word in the title of books; as, *Gibbon's Rise* and *Fall* of the *Roman Empire.* Common Nouns when personified; as,

Oh! sacred *Star* of evening, tell
In what unseen celestial sphere,
Those spirits of the perfect dwell
Too pure to rest in sadness here.

☞ Any other word that is of particular importance to the writer may begin with a capital; but the fewer of these the better.

PUNCTUATION.

The COMMA (,) is used when the sense requires a slight natural pause; as, To do good, if we have the opportunity, is our duty, and should be our happiness.

The SEMICOLON (;) marks a longer pause than the Comma, and separates clauses less closely connected; as, He that loveth pleasure shall be a poor man; he that loveth wine and oil shall not be rich.

The COLON (:) is used when the preceding part of a sentence is complete in sense and construction, and the following part is some remark naturally arising from it, given as explanation; as, Accuracy, promptness and integrity are necessary in all business transactions : there is no true success without them.   The colon is also used before examples or quotations; as, There are four seasons: Spring, Summer, Autumn, Winter.   The last words of an eminent divine were: "The best of all is, God is with us."

The PERIOD (.) is used at the close of a sentence; as, The fairest flowers are the first to fade.   The Period is also used after abbreviations; as, The oration was delivered by Rev. H. W. Beecher.

The POINT of INTERROGATION (?) is placed after every direct and complete question; as, How old is the President?   When a question is only *said to be* asked, the note of Interrogation is not used; as, The Governor General of Canada asked Prince Arthur, how he liked the Americans.

The POINT of EXCLAMATION (!) is used after expressions of sudden emotion of any kind; as, Eternity! thou pleasing, dreadful thought.

www.ingramcontent.com/pod-product-compliance
Lightning Source LLC
Chambersburg PA
CBHW031814090426
42739CB00008B/1273